DATE DUE

BRODART   Cat. No. 23-221

Cowboy Life on the Texas Plains

No. Twelve: The Centennial Series of the Association of Former Students, Texas A & M University

Ray Rector, an experienced cowboy at twenty-one years of age. "Ray Rector called himself 'The Cowboy Photographer,' a title that demonstrated his lifetime pursuit of two seemingly diverse professions. The pride and care that was the trademark of the world of the southwestern cowboy were qualities Rector carried with him into his photographic endeavors" (Roy Flukinger, Humanities Research Center, University of Texas at Austin).

Cowboy Life on the Texas Plains

The Photographs of Ray Rector

Edited by MARGARET L. RECTOR

Introduction by JOHN GRAVES

TEXAS A&M UNIVERSITY PRESS

College Station

Library of Congress Cataloging in Publication Data

Rector, Ray, 1884–1933.
    Cowboy life on the Texas plains.

       1. Ranch life—Texas—Pictorial works. 2. Cowboys—
Texas—Pictorial works. 3. Texas—Description and travel—
Views. 4. Texas—Social life and customs—Pictorial works.
I. Rector, Margaret L. (Margaret Louise), 1920–
II. Graves, John, 1920–   III. Title.
F387.R43   1982   976.4'06   82-5902
ISBN 0-89096-131-X (cloth)   AACR2
ISBN 0-89096-529-3 (paper)

Manufactured in the United States of America
SECOND PRINTING, 1992

To the memory of Ray Rector,
who had the foresight to record on film these
scenes of a passing era of Texas ranch life.

Contents

Acknowledgments

I would like to express my appreciation to Bill Witliff, Austin writer, for recognizing the value of these photographs and encouraging their documentation. He steered me to the University of Texas Humanities Research Center, which eventually became the depository for the entire collection of Ray Rector ranch photographs.

I thank my brother, Tommy Rector, for his work in reproducing all of the prints from the original negatives. Without his expertise and patience in preparing the prints, the project would never have been undertaken. I also thank my family for giving me free rein to document and publicize and find a home for the Ray Rector photographs.

My appreciation also goes to the Humanities Research Center for allowing the use of the prints for this book and for their cooperation in making my dream become a reality.

Margaret Rector

Introduction

There are a couple of main troubles with trying to say in print anything worth saying about cowboys at this belated point, though people keep trying anyhow. One is that an astounding lot has already been said about them, both by old cowboys themselves in reminiscences written or dictated late in life, and by observers of whom quite a few have been thoughtful persons with a good knowledge of the subject.

The other trouble, worse, is that the very word *cowboy*, let alone the concept, is freighted with such a load of extraneous meaning and connotation these days that any effort to furnish a new legitimate glimpse of the basic rural laborer, the "hired man on horseback" with whom the furor started, is forced to squeeze and edge and tiptoe its way around them. It is easy enough to declare at the outset that you want to consider cowboys who work with cows, not the movie-TV kind with barking pistols, or the country-music kind with longnecked beerbottles, or the currently chic designer-clad kind with styled hair, or the Dallas-football-team kind, or even the strictly rodeo kind. It's *not* easy, however, to set distance between working cowboys and the famous myth engendered from them, out of which have grown by one strange route or another all those Panavision epics, Waylon-and-Willie songs, bumper stickers extolling snuff, nine-hundred-dollar ostrich boots, and such. Nor is it easy either to separate your own thinking about working cowboys from your thinking—feeling, rather—about the myth itself, which in one or another form has a good tight

sentimental grab-hold on some part of most Americans' minds, and especially on those of Westerners.

For such reasons, I think, a good many writers, myself among them, with a Western background and an inevitable strong interest in cowboys and their world, have tended to shy away from them as a subject. There is so damned much quicksand. . . . Nevertheless, possibly spurred by an inner need to resolve the confusion for themselves, most sooner or later seem to decide they have a few words to say, a few insights to impart.

Maybe these are mine.

Even if we narrow things down to working cowboys and elbow the myth aside, at least for now, we have the initial problem of saying what a working cowboy is, and for that matter if he still exists. Obviously somebody has to brand and castrate and vaccinate and otherwise manage all those animals you still see in West Texas pastures, but if we call the ones who do it cowboys, as in the main we do, what sense can we make of the fact that during the better part of this present century, Western-minded scholars and nostalgics—and some anti-nostalgics too—have been bidding a firm farewell to the American cowboy, relegating him to history? Clearly they've been talking about something different. What they've been saying goodbye to all these years is the original model, the kind of working cowboy who participated fully in what has been called, professorially, "cowboy culture," and there is no doubt at all that he and his world are no longer with us.

That cow-camp and bunkhouse way of labor and life, with its own wry language and its values and taboos and style that have been pored over by many commentators, involved organized full crews of hired horseback professionals, men who were cowhands pure and simple. In its full-blown form it existed chiefly in connection with large cattle operations, whether owned by individual ranchers or, as frequently, by corporate bodies. Cowboying was primary, of course, on ranches of whatever size, but the bigger ones in their old shape were that life's real matrix, its framework. When the framework started to creak and sag and change, so too did the absolute cowboy way of being. It seems to me to have ended not so much with a bang as with a waning, but end it more or less did at some point within each of the varied regions of the West.

The earliest goodbye-sayers, including many old-time cow people who set down their recollections, did see it as ending with a sort of bang. In general they shared a feeling that the flavor of authentic range life had vanished with the changes barbed wire brought. Real cowboying had been knocked in the head, they were convinced, by the disappearance of the open range, the end of long trail drives and of huge roundups carried out by numbers of outfits working great tracts of unfenced country together while sorting and claiming their beasts, the heavy incursions of farmers on grassland, the replacement of half-wild longhorns with more tractable breeds of cattle, the inclusion in ranch work of unequestrian jobs like patching fences and greasing windmills, and so on.

Many who write on the subject still see its history thus. I guess it depends on definitions. . . . Certainly the waning commenced back there when wire fences started doing away with the frontier concept of grass as anyone's property who had some cows to eat it. Plenty of big operations collapsed at that time, a full century ago, and in the decades that ensued, bigness and its ways stayed under siege as generations of new owners and investors found out for themselves what stubborn family-scale ranchers have forever known to be true: that ranching most of the time, in terms of return against the value of holdings, is a tricky and often comical business proposition. Huge expanses of the best parts of the prairies and plains did go under the plow, and the cattle empire did for the most part dwindle back rather soon to the sort of country the Old World in its hard-won wisdom had always assigned to grazing use—wasteland in farmers' eyes, rough or rocky or arid or otherwise unfit for cultivation. Graziers would never again on this planet have so wide and rich a realm to exploit as they had known on the American plains before the coming of wire, nor would their cowboys ever again lead so pure and untrammeled a herding life.

Nevertheless the West has an enormous lot of rough and rocky and arid land in it, and any Westerner past fifty or sixty, with an eye for rural things, knows that full-plumage cultural cowboys, while diminishing in numbers and prominence, were with us for a good while after that main change occurred. From my own observations, which have been neither intimate nor learned nor steadily sustained, I'd put their demise at the approximate point when good-sized ranches started finding cowboy culture uneconomic, and I think that point was reached here in Texas at about the watershed time of the Second World War, which, like the First one before it and the Civil one before that, brought an end to many things.

That old range life in its wholeness was masculine and bachelor and physical in tone, shaped around the work done together—or alone, for that matter, in many of the tasks—by skilled men without much property beyond clothes and bedding and saddles. It was in truth rather monastic within the work itself, incongruous though the word may be in relation to the majority of such men. Many were drifters from job to job as personal whim or seasonal layoffs dictated, while others—more, probably, as time went on—might stay on at one outfit for years or for life and acquire such accouterments as wives and kids. Some, in fact, like the black hands found on the upper Texas coastal prairies and the brown ones at home in the South Texas brush and through much of the border country to the Pacific, were often tied in place by social forces or feudal preference and might well have been born on the land where they cowboyed all their lives. Whoever and wherever they were, though, and whatever they were like as individuals or ethnic enclaves, the abilities they were required to have were similar, and it was basic to the values they held in common, their culture if you like, that on a given range at a given time their responsibilities were toward the works' aims and toward one another, and not toward too much else.

These traditional crews laboring in traditional ways could do all that needed to be done each year with an operation's livestock, using ropes, horses, muscles, and an intricate accumulation of adeptnesses and cow lore that had come down to them in large part from colonial Mexico. Anybody who got to see them functioning, as I and a good many other youngsters of my generation were sometimes privileged to do, knows that barbed wire had not changed them radically. Long after fenced ranges became the rule, their working life still often revolved around such Old West institutions as remudas, camps and chuckwagons and crusty cooks, personal honor feistily maintained, rawhide horseplay, roundups, and in some sections even occasional trail drives across country to a railroad shipping point or another ranch.

Thus a top hand from the open-range 1870s, trans-planted by time machine to a West Texas roundup cow camp in, say, 1930, might have found himself somewhat cramped by the scale of things but not too badly off base. He would have noted fashion changes in the way men's hair was cut and the slang they used and the shape of their hats and saddletrees. In gentle country he might have been startled by the arrival of automobiles bearing ranch bigwigs and spectactors, sometimes female. He would have observed that the horses were bigger and better-looking than most he'd gotten to ride, and the cattle mainly less snuffy and in consequence easier to handle. His eye accustomed to virgin country would have seen clearly that six decades of heavy grazing and erosion had played much hell with the grass, bringing in more brush and weeds and baring more rocks and gouging gullies. He would have been fed and paid a little better, most likely, though cowhands' wages were still unimpressive for the abilities and labor involved.

But the job itself and the men would have been the job and men he knew. On ranches where a pasture to be worked might be fifteen or twenty thousand acres in size and a day's ride away from headquarters, what there was to do and how it was accomplished had not altered much. If here in Texas—and I suspect in most other parts of the West—World War II tolled the final knell of this way of living and working in its typical big-ranch form, the remarkable thing to a sidelines observer like me is not its ending but its long survival, a proud, dexterous, manual and horseback manner of doing things, spread around a great region, that endured in places where conditions were right, through at least the fourth decade of this most technological of centuries. That is pretty fair cultural durability in a changeful country like ours. The antebellum cotton South in all its cherished new-rich glory did not last any longer, though of course it did end with a very definitive bang.

The main things that relegated this kind of cowboying to the picturesque past are clear enough. One was harder times than usual for ranches big or little during the droughty Depression years and after, leading to the break-up or shrinkage of many and heavy retrenchment on others, unless, as sometimes in Texas, the discovery of petroleum bailed them out. Another was a general national postwar emphasis on doing away with old labor-intensive methods, stimulated in part by rising expectations as to pay and hours and work conditions on the part of labor itself, even including cowboys. There was, in addition, the vast rapid growth of cities and the drift toward them of all kinds of country people, though in terms of the cattle country it's hard to say whether this was a cause or an effect of the general push toward change.

The practices that began supplanting the old way were rather simple ones, most of them in some use in the 1920s and '30s, that got a better toehold when the war made good cheap hired help scarce, then spread and became standard procedure in the years that followed. This was because they were now less costly than camps and big crews and chuckwagons and numerous horses, in a time during which the cattle trade found itself sharing meagerly, when at all, in the frenetic extended national boom, and for survival its practitioners had to seek out ways to whittle expenses.

In essence the new way consisted of efficient corrals, smaller pastures, and the motorized transport of men and animals. Not much, it would seem, but enough to sound that knell. . . . If, at strategic spots on your ranch—how many spots depending on its size—you build well-designed sets of pens with holding areas, working chutes and alleys, and cutting gates, and you equip them with patent headgates or squeeze chutes or calf-tables to immobilize animals for branding, dehorning, castration, inoculation, and treatment of their ills, you will have wrought a fundamental change. You have established in each such set of pens a sort of assembly-line theater of cattle management where three to five fairly capable men, most of them on foot, can do in a day the work that may formerly have needed three or four times that number of highly trained hands and a good many first-rate horses, cutting out and roping and flanking and throwing beasts and holding them down in the good old-fashioned way. You've also done away with a whole slew of lovely complex activity, and have disgruntled all true cowboys. But you've saved a slew of money, too, even considering the cost of the pens and chutes and the new fences that feed cattle to them without half the rounding up and driving that used to have to be done.

I had a good friend, a redheaded rancher now dead, who was manager and through inheritance part-owner of an eleven- or twelve-hundred-cow operation, not big as big used to go in the West but sizable enough to have maintained a smallish crew of pure cultural cowboys in the times when that way prevailed. He was not entirely typical of his breed, being one of the best-read and most restlessly inquiring people I've known, but he took cattle seriously enough. On occasion he would maintain stoutly, and in his drinking days rather fiercely, that the old way when practiced with art and restraint was far easier on animals, inflicting less trauma and loss of weight—the latter a stud bugaboo of ranchers from early times onward, because weight is what they get paid for. Since he'd had experience with both ways and was not a very sentimental sort, I assume that he was right. But even he had long since gone over to working his beasts in chutes, through sordid economics.

Pickups and trailers to carry hands with their mounts to the work after breakfast, returning them home to warm beds and wives at night, have pretty much done away with long rides, camps, and the monastic bachelor tone of cow work, even where cowboy skills still get a good bit of use. A changeover from railroads to big trailer trucks for hauling large numbers of cattle, straight from corrals to wherever they're being sent, has subtracted its measure of colorful action also. Both, along with the use of chute-equipped pens, have greatly reduced the number of men and horses a ranch has to keep and pay and feed and the amount of riding that surviving hands find it needful to do, at least outside of the roughest mountain sections. I haven't in many years, for instance, noticed in this region a young or middle-aged man with true bandy legs of the sort that some older cowboys used to roll around on when afoot, a proud deformity acquired from years of spending most daylight hours, besides a good many at night, astraddle a round-barreled four-legged friend or sometimes enemy. I've seen young, goat-roping, snuff-dipping, rodeo-aspirant types walking with legs bowed out on purpose, and very prettily traditional it is, but that is somehow different.

The few real cowboys of the old stamp whom I've known fairly well, I've known mainly as individual older men here and there over a period of decades, coming on them dehorsed in jobs at filling stations or grocery stores or boarding stables, or retired, or sometimes elevated to the economy's more respected strata. They were a varied lot, and nearly all I've kept track of have died by now. Only a couple of them had spent their whole working lives with horses and cattle, the rest having cowboyed for a few years or maybe a decade or more in youth before something— changing times, restlessness, ambition, an accumulation of stiffnesses and injuries, marriage to some girl aspiring to fancier things than life in a ranch hand's stark cottage— had led them into other paths.

Some would let you know about that background right away, while with others you learned of it accidentally, perhaps from somebody else. Even so, having been cowboys tended to loom as a central fact in their recollections, and they spoke most easily and humorously concerning its details with others who had that central memory also and a right to talk about it. On the infrequent occasions when I heard such talk I was reminded of the way old marines talk together, or old fighter pilots, or others sharing a past young-bachelor swatch of life they see as proud and special.

If these aging types had a few qualities in common besides just human nature, the qualities probably did have some relation to the thing they had all once been, unless I've read that connection into my remembrance of them. Most salient, I believe, was that none was truly a slob. One or two were pretty alcoholic by the time I got to know them, and a couple had some seized-up neurons and arterioles beneath their skulls, but those are other matters. . . . Whatever they did for pleasure or gain, most tended to do it deftly and with flair, caring about getting it right and making it look easy, in the way that a good roper's throws with a lariat may look easy to unversed onlookers. It was a sort of athlete's attitude, and I believe they'd all have made good to excellent game-players in their time if chasing various kinds of balls had mattered as much back then as it seems to now.

Born in rural times and mostly in rural places, they were fairly unanimous in a queasiness concerning remembered cotton patches, milk cows, flatulent mules, and iron-handed fathers. Only one had grown up in real ranch country, though others, raised on mixed farming-and-stockraising family places of the sort that used to characterize much of central and near-west Texas, had carried some basic cowboy knowledge with them when they'd decamped toward wider horizons. The rest seemed to have carried mainly a sour resolve to put miles between themselves and plows and cotton sacks as they moved toward that looser and freer Western life whose legend they'd already absorbed.

Seldom rooted in the places where they now lived, deficient for the most part in institutional loyalties, they valued friendship and tended to judge met strangers swiftly and directly and permanently—and often, for that matter, unfairly. I don't think many of them cared much about money and position, and in consequence they usually had little of either, though on the other hand some had adapted to current reality and had learned to care very much.

The bulk of those whom I knew were Texans by birth and had done their cowboying chiefly in the state, some having worked on the Matadors or the Swensons or others of the old, large, established outfits in the Rolling Plains and beyond, but most on more modest if still substantial spreads. A few had wandered farther. My favorite of the lot, a real friend who died in his eighties some years ago, had left his family's place south of Waco at eighteen and had cowboyed his way to Montana where he worked on several ranches, got drunk more than once with Charles M. Russell, and joined the Buffalo Bill Wild West Show in its latter years. He could deliver verbatim the speech that Colonel Cody, as he always called him, had made to introduce the Pony Express act in which he himself had ridden, and he had performed in the Roman Relays, one foot on each of two running horses, in Madison Square Garden in New York. Later he'd worked on a California ranch that furnished livestock for early Western movies, and had done stunt work there with Yakima Canutt and played on Will Rogers' cowboy polo team. He had, in short, heard the owl hoot in a good many different places and had led a hell of a life for a country boy from the Blacklands. And though by habit he spoke little of himself, he knew it had all been fine and if he liked you he'd tell you about it, in the little shotgun rent house where he lived in his last years, raising large perfect tomatoes in five-gallon cans half full of horse manure.

The joy that was still in him—and in most cowboys, I

think, even when you couldn't see it—was somehow epitomized in a browned, creased, Kodak snapshot he once showed me of himself when young on a big black horse by a spruce-bordered mountain lake, wearing a high-crowned Stetson and bearskin chaps, grinning like a possum, and clearly on top of his world. The picture had in it the springtime feel of a passage I love in that most light-heartedly honest of cowboy books, E. C. Abbott's *We Pointed Them North*: "And besides, I never had time to gamble; I couldn't sit still long enough; I always had to be up, talking, singing, drinking at the bar. I was so happy and full of life, I used to feel, when I got a little whiskey inside me, that I could jump twenty feet in the air. I'd like to go back and feel that way once more. If I could go back I wouldn't change any of it."

Abbott's career dated back to open-range days, and the old ones with whom I was friendly had all functioned quite a bit later than that. But I don't believe many of them would have changed "it" very much either, any of it outside of some ill-knit bones and hernias and mashed prostates and such, and even those some were proud of in a perverse and stove-up way.

So I suppose that what my own personal perception of generalized cowboy character comes down to, as manifested in those few old-timers I've known, is mainly its strong flavor of dexterity and joy and pride. Cowboys of this original breed were genuinely competent at horsemanship and roping and the other elements of their trade, because they had to be competent in order merely to get jobs and keep them, and to gain the acceptance of the men they worked with. Some had extra-special talent with ropes or rough horses or whatnot—tales about such were legion—but all had basic skill and knowledge. Most for that matter had probably been to some degree "naturals" to begin with, because if they hadn't been the sort of youths who learned physical things rapidly and well, and hadn't had a capacity for making the varied snap decisions that range cow work entails, they wouldn't have been allowed to become the thing they were. Instead they would most likely have joined the swarms of other young would-be buckaroos for whom the legend had not jelled, and who'd drifted back home to the cotton patch or ended in strange cities somewhere, not having made the grade. It was, as Walter Prescott Webb once noted, a process of natural selection, based not only on physical deftness and quickly acquisitive brains but also on such ancient virtues as guts and reliability.

Cowhands were thus an elite, and like all elites were proud. And being proud and mainly young, most derived a lot of sheer fun from the life they led, as if it had been play. Work *is* play, in truth, if you like it and do it well, though I expect a majority of cowboys would have been ready for a fist-fight if they'd heard described as play their customary labor. Nevertheless it's clear they took exultant pleasure and pride not only in its dexterous good parts but even in its worst ones. Pride in staying begrimed and sweaty and whiskeyless and womanless for however long a piece of work took, through days on days of twelve or fifteen hours or more devoted to the pursuit and management of the dim-witted recalcitrant creatures from which they took their name. Pride in the quantity of dust they breathed, in not only riding but making good use of horses that were sometimes only half broken to the work, in getting front teeth kicked out by calves, in the coarse heavy food they gulped down at intervals, in enduring such weather as presented itself with a minimum of raiment and shelter, in flopping down at night on the ground for a few hours of itchy, coughing sleep before being waked in the dark to start again. Less pride, maybe, in ripping up hands and forearms while stretching fence wire, in getting dizzy forty feet up in the air while messing with a windmill's gear box, or in doctoring cattle's foul wounds in a bad screw-worm year, but those were parts of the whole.

The work had to give such pride and pleasure, I think. If it hadn't, why else would quick and capable young men have stuck with it, for range-cook grub and wages of thirty or forty or fifty dollars a month or whatever the times were paying? In point of fact, I suspect these men's delight in doing what they did for a living, with their resultant willingness to do it for peanut pay, probably was a main reason the old way of working cattle survived past its logical time. It kept that way economic. Up through the 1930s, in much of the West, it furnished ranches with a steady supply of what were in a sense trained young slave workers, slaves not to the ranches themselves but to their own happy satisfaction in being good at what they did, and to their love for it. And if very often they hid all that behind a dry, laconic manner with which, like many elites, they sought to convey an impression that they didn't give a damn, this was practically all front. They gave a damn, all right. It was why they were there.

Cowboys, then, were all noble fellows? It would be nice to think so. Guts and reliability and happy proud competence, after all, are powerfully attractive attributes in the eyes of most of us, especially when possessed by a horseback figure at home in big country who reminds us, not wrongly, of a time on this continent when freedom could be a literal and physical thing. So attractive in fact that the simplest, most popular form of the cowboy myth, which started abuilding almost as soon as the plains cattle industry itself, did decree very early that cowboys indeed *were* noble, endowed as a class with more or less of those virtues listed in the Boy Scout Code. Quaint in aspect and language, yes, and varied enough in personality to merit salty nicknames and provide color in pulp-magazine stories and dime novels and—later on—films, but clean-

17

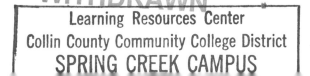

minded, true, good-hearted types, every one. If they went bad they did it whole hog and stopped being cowboys, turning instead into rustlers or stagecoach robbers or hired gunfighters or other typified miscreants within the myth.

I believe my own earliest and perhaps healthiest intimation that there was something wrong with this premise, that cowboys were human along with the rest of us, came when I was about ten and saw a particular cowboy on a Fort Worth street. I was in a car with some adults, passing small ratty hotels and cafés near the intersection of North Main and Exchange Avenue. It was a period when the stockyards and auctions and packing plants of that neighborhood were operating full tilt, and nearly all the people you saw there made their livings from cattle or swine or horses or mules—buying them, selling them, sledge-hammering them in the head, cutting them into pieces, bringing them to town for sale or slaughter, or shipping bought ones back to ranches and farms. Since the area was permanently overhung by an intense odor compounded of manure and urine and packing-house offal, people from other parts of Fort Worth usually went there only on business, though when big winds blew out of Canada in winter the North Side smell permeated the whole city and reminded us of our heritage. In itself that aroma should have served as a sound defense against the cowboy myth's effects, nobility and romance being very hard to associate with it.

Nonetheless most of us kids of that time and place did participate in the national fondness for the myth, our primary enthusiasm at the moment being directed toward a rock-jawed, straight-shooting cowboy movie star called Tom Mix. He had a horse known as Tony in whose honor, I would judge, about a quarter of the Shetland ponies in the state of Texas were then named. Nor did we usually have much trouble in squaring our feeling about this ster-ling figure with the fact that we lived close to cattle country, knowing or being kin to people with cowboy pasts or other cow-business connections. The city's annual rodeo was a good one, and while I suppose there were some full-time professional contestants even then, most came from the ranks of plain ranch cowhands. If fortunate, we'd been taken to visit ranches and we knew already that what was most special about real cowboys was the beautiful, violent, skillful work that they and their horses performed. But we awarded them their full share of Tom Mix's romance and nobility too, and if we spent about as much time trying to lay a loop on dogs, one another, and passing cars' headlights with lengths of clothesline rope as we did in cap-gun duels and wars, it all fitted together comfortably in our minds.

The cowboy I saw on the curb of North Main Street that day looked remarkably like Tom Mix, with a good big jaw and an aquiline nose and even a hank of dark hair falling across his forehead from beneath a pushed-back Stetson. I knew what he was because in those departed, naïve days practically nobody but ranch hands and their employers wore boots and big hats in town, where it was generally felt that only they had the right. This cowboy was not, however, acting like the Tom Mix I'd known. He was unmistakably hog drunk, and was hanging onto an iron street-sign post with both hands while he vomited partly in the gutter and partly on himself, having recently, it appeared, ingested some chili with beans. . . .

I had seen drunks before and found them mainly comic, as children often do. This one wasn't funny to me, though. Shuddering, miserably pale and lorn and alone in that miasmal North Side air to which he'd just contributed his mite, he stared up toward our slow-moving car out of bloodshot eyes from which retch-tears coursed down his cheeks. I stared back and felt reality squirm in my mind. The myth didn't perish for me in that moment of comprehension, and if the poor devil hadn't looked like Tom Mix it might not have mattered at all. But I somehow never afterward felt quite so smitten by old Tom and his Tony, or indeed by any other members of the movie-cowboy species who showed up over the years.

That desolated reveller, I suppose, was the obverse side of Teddy Blue Abbott's thinking he could jump twenty feet in the air. Maybe he himself had felt that way a couple of hours before. Farther along in life I was to find out for myself that blowoff fun, which seeks to exaggerate joy, is more frequently obverse than not, though if you're young and male and full of yourself in a certain raunchy and innocent way you go back to it time and again, hoping for one of the occasions when it does turn out right. And if you were a young cowhand, blowoff fun was likely to be where you sought, when you could, surcease from all that happy, grueling cow work. There was nothing surprising in this, but little that was noble, either. Distant for the most part from bright lights and liquor and compliant females, locked into a system of labor that furnished no vacations and not even many days off, you tried to make the most of what free time you got, and—I judge from observation and from unproud personal remembrance—very often flubbed it in the execution and ended up like that Tom Mix cowboy, sickly plastered and clutching a signpost or a tree somewhere. Or clutching a barroom antagonist who'd just fisted your face to red mush. Or clutching, more fondly but not more romantically or nobly, one of the sagging, foulmouthed, perhaps golden-hearted women I used to see cowboys with, later when I knew what the women were, in that same stockyards section.

Not being one who gets much thrill from fulmination, I see little point in waxing censorious over other disparities between cowboy reality and the more high-flown claims of the myth, though a couple might be pointed out. Like most other physically excellent, elite-minded young men found in groups—marines, athletes, whatever—cowboys were intolerant of difference and seem to have been fairly often unbearable in relation to people from outside their own little world, at any rate when there were enough of them around to keep their group-feeling fueled and to make the unbearableness stick. In the old accounts the results usually pass as humor, and I guess they were, though somewhere along the path of later life I myself seem to have lost a sense of the full hilarity of such antics as yanking off a timorous stranger's small urban hat on the street and shooting it full of holes on the pretext that it was dangerous, while cawing laughter rang all around.

As for the myth's usual rigid moral separation of the good guys from the bad, I have more than once or twice heard old hands speak with humorous affection, approaching admiration, about certain cattle thieves they'd known, cowboys like themselves who had decided to better their lot by the direct and simple method of abstracting riches from the rich, and who may have gone back to competent cowboying afterward if their efforts led to neither affluence nor durance vile. It's worth noting also that the popularity of some desperadoes and hard-riding bank and train robbers was at its stoutest around range cookfires. For cowboys—tough, skillful, elite brotherhood though they may have been—were among the world's exploited have-nots, and have-nots on the whole, alas, have ever relished lawless heroes who disgruntle staid and moneyed folk, even if few of them may choose to disgruntle such folk for themselves.

A larger quibble about the mythic nobility of cowboys and ranchers and their world and its ways has been surfacing now and then in recent years and has to do with current awareness of ecological values. It is based, of course, on hindsight. Illustrative of it, perhaps, is a complaint I saw leveled not long ago at Andy Adams' well-known *The Log of a Cowboy*, published early in this century as the fictional account of a five-month trail drive from the Mexican border to Montana in 1882, and based closely on the author's own working experience. Though without literary pretension, this is an immensely authentic piece of work, probably the most authentic on its subject, and the writer of the essay I read recognizes its worth. This serves, however, to swell his irritation that it is, in his view, needlessly marred by the inclusion near its end of an extended brutal scene involving a female bear. Adams' trail hands happen on this animal eating berries with her two cubs, rope her into snarling helplessness, and proceed happily to shoot her to pieces as well as killing the cubs, not to eat or for self-protection but just for the high hell of it. "When we met at the wagon for dinner," says the narrator, ". . . the hunt was unanimously voted the most exciting bit of sport and powder burning we had experienced on our trip."

Probably most people nowadays with any sense of how natural things mesh and link and dovetail, and any knowledge of how those patterns have been savaged on this continent—as well as on all the others—would read that episode with something of an inward wince. Yet if Adams had left it out of the picture he was painting of cowboy life, there would have been a big hole in the fabric of truth he was trying to weave. Spawned of the frontier that saw nature less as mother than as enemy when not source of wealth, cowboys in general (yes, we're still generalizing, maybe a hair too hard) were unecological exemplars of what Wallace Stegner has described as the West's curious urge to destroy itself. They stayed that way too, for about as long as they were around in anything resembling the old form, despite their affection for the kind of wide country they knew and their nostalgia for its lost virginity. For many of them, if something moved and didn't moo or neigh or carry a brand, you shot it, or pulped it with a rock or a stick, or strychnined it, or roped it and dragged it to

death, and afterward maybe you felt so good about this that you hung it up on a fence by a road. Edible carcasses were most often hauled in for consumption, but edibility wasn't the point. The point was raising cattle and imposing human purpose on the land, and the traditional and easy way to view wildlife was either as irrelevant to that point or else as a threat to it, preferably the latter since it lent virtue to killing.

One of my best and brightest friends, though we live far apart these days and see each other seldom, absconded from a city home at the age of thirteen in the mid–late 1930s and made his way to Wyoming, where against the odds he earned acceptance as a "button" on a good ranch and was well on his way to full cowhand status when World War II began and he joined up. He told me once about a thing that happened after he was discharged from the service and went back to those haunts, finding old cowboy compadres there with a war behind them too and an itch for simple pleasures. They got hold of a war-surplus jeep and a jug of something corrosive and went cruising about the sagebrush, looking for things to shoot. Spotting a fleeing herd of antelope on fairly even ground, they charged and got among them at thirty-five or forty miles an hour and started firing at random. By the time I knew him he'd moved around in the world quite a lot and had started using his first-rate mind, and he felt some slight shame about the memory. But there'd been no shame in that jeep, only exhilaration. "You wouldn't believe what a time we had," he said. "We slaughtered those fast bastards right and left."

Cowboys, then, were all *ig*noble fellows? You might think so if you looked only at their less sterling traits. But you might yet more easily think the same thing about humanity in general if you looked at it in the same way. I fear the main point to bear in mind is—still and again—that cowboys *were* ineluctably human like the rest of us, in view of which slightly unsavory fact their commonly held virtues, quite real ones, may have been perhaps the more impressive. Even that gaily lethal attitude they so often demonstrated toward wild and natural things is flatly human, I believe, emphasized though it may have been in frontiersmen and cowboys by the opportunities furnished them by their times, their surroundings, and the tools and weapons at hand. But to follow out the ramifications of that thought would lead us into avenues distant from the subject of happy cowboys. . . . Let us note in dismissal of the topic that a good bit of this cowboy destructiveness derived less from murderous whim than from what had to be done, at least if animal husbandry of the Western sort was going to become the main use of all that land not suited for farming, which history decreed should be so. Livestock do not thrive, for instance, in the presence of such predators as lobo wolves and cougars and grizzly bears, nor did the cow crowd have an appreciative view of rattlesnakes or even such timorous beasties as prairie dogs, with their multitudinous burrows that fractured running horses' legs and cartwheeled riders through the sunlit air to collision with earth and stone. And if a lot of us now think we might have been less harsh on the scheme of things, the fact is that environmental hindsight has its own myth of nobility.

I confess to a sneaking, lingering, personal fondness for the cowboy myth, and to an ambivalence concerning it. For those of us who grew up knowing a little about cattle and real ranches, the myth came in at least two flavors. One was the widely popular, usually puerile, dime-thriller-and-Tom-Mix thing based on derring-do, while the other, less commercialized and closer to reality though just about as simpleminded at times, involved an exaggeration of the virtues and skills displayed by cowboys at work. As I've noted, youngsters of my time here in Texas had little trouble in mixing the two and thus fabricating for themselves a somewhat more entire myth, compounded of cap guns and Shetland ponies and cotton clothesline lariats. And if a really powerful use of the myth in the form of a book or a film is ever achieved, I expect it will do very much the same thing in adult terms.

I haven't seen it done yet, but neither have I seen everything that's been done. It does seem clear that rendition of the wide or popular myth of Colt pistols and fair ladies has much improved in quality in recent years as it has gained in complexity, with, for instance, occasional noble farmers or noble Indians being awarded as much heroic stature as cowboys and cavalrymen and such, sometimes more. On a more elevated level the pop myth has been subjected to some quite good high-comic spoofs, and now and again also, writers and moviemakers have been coming up with work, still discernibly mythic in point and framework, that has legitimate force and sometimes comes close to getting hold of the feel of things as they probably were, even while usually continuing to evade or ignore the real cowboy reason for being, the hard, graceful, constant work.

Maybe a case could be made for rodeo in its present professional manifestation as a supplementary pop myth that takes care of that side of things. A much sounder case, however, and in terms of more genuine myth, could be made for the painting and sculpture of the better Western artists from Remington and Russell on, where range labor in all its varied, violent color, the physical interplay of men and horses and cattle and country, is very often a main focus, dealt with for its own sake. Artists like that, whether or not they've had a whole vision of the West as it was, have known quite well what cowboys consisted of.

Valid artistic presentation of either side of the myth brings in another dimension, of course, and it may be objected that when something becomes art—i.e., truth powerfully rendered—it ceases to be myth. But that comfortable separation only works if you define myth in its cheapest sense, that of pure falsification, which isn't real myth at all. I possess neither the scholarship nor the desire to go deeply into this subject, but it's something that anyone who tries to set things down right, on paper or canvas or wherever, has had to think about. Art and myth and truth and life are snakishly entangled. Art does deal essentially with the true, myth with the ideal—and behind even the ingrained commercial purpose, the constant idiotic mayhem, the misapprehension of fact, the childish and puritan twisting of motives and conduct of the pop cowboy myth at its worst, there does lurk a set of ideals of honesty and courage and staunchness and other basic virtues.

But art concerns itself with the ideal as well—if only, sometimes, with its absence—and while the possibilities for esthetic argument are endless, I doubt many of us believe that the value, as art, of a piece of bronze buckingbronco sculpture is lessened by the fact that it may convey an ideal of cowboy guts and skill, perhaps more guts and skill than most real cowboys had. It may or may not be lousy art; much Western stuff fails through the same sentimental distortion and misfired talent that devil artists everywhere. But if it is lousy, the fact that an element of the ideal is present is not the reason. Art can thus become myth, or myth become art, so that many times it's not possible to say which is which. . . .

Another curious point is that myth can influence the direction of human life, as can art, and may even influence its live subject matter if the timing is right. The popular cowboy myth was not shaped for cowboys, but for (and in a sense by) a non-Western public, worldwide in extent as time passed, which seized on it with a passion that could only have come from deep need. But it reached real cowboys as well, the later ranch-working kind, and they seized on it too—some of them, indeed, having left home to get to be cowboys on account of its potent pull. It is well known that much of the favorite reading matter around chuckwagons and bunkhouses was pulp Western fiction, and when cowboy movies started being shown in towns across the cattle country their audiences included plenty of men who might guffaw and slap their legs over technical bloopers involving animals or the details of work and language—might in fact grouse bitterly about them later—but who soaked up the messages just about as appreciatively as any Philadelphian. Passing by the question of possibly reinforced egotism, what this appears to mean is that the myth, operating with a sort of reverse English on it, entered and reentered them and flavored their perception of what they were. Maybe it made some of them a bit pop-mythic themselves, if anybody can be. Ideals not being intended to serve as laws, but as reference points. . . .

It may well be simpleminded of me, but I admit I have a hard time seeing this as always bad, whether or not the myth involved is pure and true. No doubt it can sometimes lead to posing and self-worship and trying to be one's own grandfather and the like, as it did in the maudlin, alcoholic Panhandle protagonist, not a favorite of Texans, of Jane Kramer's acidly anti-mythic *The Last Cowboy*. But myself, I find it quite pleasant to consider that that poor drunk Tom Mix figure of my youth, yorking publicly into a gutter on North Main Street in Fort Worth, may have had the cinematic Tom's sterling presence working inside him as an antidote to degradation. Just as some kid bouncing a pickup across a pasture today in, say, Borden County, Texas, hauling feed cubes to steers and checking heifers for calving trouble, mooning about a girl with whom he nearly made it last night, can have a hunk of both Charlie Russell and John Wayne in his soul and is undoubtedly better off for it—nobler, by God, if you like.

Then, for that matter, there's history—including such

things as memoirs, and honest photographs snapped in time to put old ways on record—which seldom overlaps with myth except to report it, but can be art if it's good enough or, if it's not, can serve as art's (and thus myth's) prime subject matter. Let us not, however, ride our pinto ponies any farther down that analytical trail. . . .

There is no doubt that the myth in both its forms got its hooks into my own psyche when I was young, and that some traces of its influence still remain there despite the countervailing effects of experience and of a lifelong effort as a writer, maybe vain, to arrive at facts and truths unsentimentally. I am in no sense a cowboy and never got close to becoming one. What little illusion I ever attained in that respect came sporadically during adolescence on what the big-ranch cowboys would have called shirttail outfits, small operations where farming might loom as large as cattle in the scheme of things. It consisted of being allowed sometimes to ride out and help drive animals in for working or shipping, getting to wrestle a few calves now and then, and being tricked aboard an occasional unfriendly horse with results that usually satisfied the hopes of whoever it was that had tricked me.

Notwithstanding this unheroic cowboy past of mine, these days I find myself living in cattle country by choice and for about two decades now I've run a small, not highly profitable herd of Angus and crossbred beef cows under stock-farm conditions, doing the work that needs to be done with them and liking practically all of it outside of a few obstetrical crises. This atavism in me, if that's what it is, is not a simple thing and it comes from no single source, but I'm aware that it has at least some slight connection with those fragments of the myth still lodged in me like shards of an old grenade, even if an observer of our methods might have a hard time seeing this. We deal with our calves in a chute with a headgate, and are so far removed from the ki-yi-yippee side of things that we usually toll beasts to the corral with rattling buckets of feed, unless they're sullen from recent handling and have to have their minds changed by my daughter on her mare. The only real cowboy aptitude for which I can discern a lingering juvenile yen in myself is the ability to throw a rope with a fair certainty of catching a creature in motion, but I hardly ever seem to feel impelled to try it any more.

Something down inside me, though, would still have liked to be one. A cowboy is not the only thing that some part of me would have liked to be, but it's one of them. Not at this point Tom Mix, not the Virginian or the Lone Ranger or any other of their virtuous ilk. Not even good, solid, lately departed John Wayne, himself damned nearly a work of art. Just a competent friend of Teddy Blue Abbott's, say, or one of those lean and weathered types riding rough wild country in a Russell painting, in that simpler time when freedom could be a literal and physical thing for proud, tough, dexterous, reliable men on horseback. Or so at least that something inside me, and inside a lot of other people, does profoundly wish to believe.

So we shall not look upon their like again, or look again at any rate upon the like of those weathered fellows who lived the cowboy life whole. Shall we then add our verse to the somewhat dissonant chorus which over the years, with asperity or irony or praise, has been saying farewell? Goodbye, American Cowboy: is that our message too?

To a fat extent it has to be, I guess. The old ones are as finally gone as the wild red men that went away before them, and in the kind of world we have on hand, even in the West where all that land you can't farm is still mainly used by cows, what remains of that way of being seems ever less relevant to wherever it is that we're headed. Its skills and lore have been abraded by economics and chutes and pickup trucks, and maybe more importantly, the romantic pull it once had for young recruits, its glamor so to speak, is being sucked away elsewhere, partly by the old myth itself and some offspring it has spawned.

There is glamor enough, for instance, in big-time rodeo, where some of the old skills, plus others that have no range use, are brilliantly employed in ritual form for the pleasure of a growing and avid public. But rodeo is increasingly show business and its successful "cowboy" participants are increasingly professionals—athletes, performers, whatever you want to call them—whose connection with the management of beef cattle on grassland, when it exists at all, runs second to the pull of the arena's acclaim and its cash and the tightly cowgirl-clad groupies at beerhall and motel-room parties after the show. More and more the sort of youngsters who once might have wanted to be the real thing are yearning toward that world instead, taking jobs sometimes on ranches for a living and for experience while they wait to break into the money and the glory. A man I knew who ranched in New Mexico had to furlough two of his three hands, one a Navaho, whenever the season for certain rodeos rolled around. He would have lost them otherwise. Neither ever won anything to brag about, but they had to hang onto the illusion that they might. With a slightly paranoid note in his voice, he claimed they also knocked weight off his calves by running and roping them for practice when he wasn't around.

There is glamor too, with far less connection to the old cowboy way of being, in some other things—in, for instance, wearing two or three thousand bucks' worth of custom-made Western clothes (or, alternatively, forty bucks' worth of very scruffy ones) while you sing into a microphone and pluck on your guitar, or in just wearing that kind of clothes out for a night on the town in Dallas or Houston or, according to report, New York. And this glamor like the rodeo kind has been inherited in part,

however deviously, from that tough, adept, monastic, ever more dimly envisioned old brotherhood of the cow camps, leaving precious little of the stuff for any yahoo throwback who just wants to live out where it's lonesome and take care of cows for a meager wage—as, incredibly, some still do.

Because that's the hitch in saying with assurance goodbye, American Cowboy, goodbye. About the time you've put your farewell speech together in your head and have started waving a bandanna toward that lone, lean, mounted figure crossing a hogback ridge into the sunset, another cowboy, maybe not a cultural member of the vanished brotherhood but tough and able and legitimate nonetheless, may very well ease up inquisitively beside you and say, "What the hell are you doin'?"

You have to define him and recognize him for yourself, I guess, and he may be in a pickup or on a tractor when you first see him, though it's not where he looks best. He's not hard to find in Texas if you look in the right places, though for me he popped up most recently in Wyoming last fall, where I'd gone to cast a few flies for trout before cold weather set in. The ranch I was visiting lies among the foothills and the worn-down, sculptured peaks of an ancient range east of the Rockies, and these days only steers are run on it, being bought as big calves in the spring, grazed all summer on the mineral-strong mountain grass, and sold when autumn comes at a profit, if any, which derives from the three hundred pounds or more each animal can gain in that time. Because of market ups and downs this kind of ranching has a strong element of gambling in it, but it gets around the heavy winter feeding and care required with cow-calf operations in northern country. Absentee-owned, the ranch is run by a foreman and his wife with help from two or three seasonal hands in the months when the steers are there, and during the time of my visit they were bringing animals down from the higher country and assembling them for shipping.

A couple of nearby ranchers came to pitch in as well, bringing along hired hands or wives and horses, and the size and makeup of the small working crew varied from day to day according to what different ones of them found had to be done at home. Such neighboring-up for main jobs, by people who know they'll all be thus helped in their turns, is a time-hallowed institution in cow country, especially where family-sized operations are common. Working ten- and twelve-hour days during which they covered a given tract of country and gathered up its steers, they knew the land's shape and knew one another, and the way they functioned together was pretty to see as they were coming in at evening or, occasionally, when I could watch them during the day in some valley whose creek I was fishing. Mainly it wasn't elaborate cowboy work, just herding, but in that intricately up-and-down terrain, with beasts that were spooky and stubborn from living five fat months on their own, it was fancier—more picturesque, anyhow—than what you usually see in rolling Texas in these degenerate times, with a good bit of hard, fast riding and cutting and heading off, and more rarely a little rope work with some part-Brahman outlaw that had to be choked down or busted to convince him that the herd's winding route of march was the appropriate one for him too.

They were efficient rather than showy in the way they did things, and a couple of the women were about as good as most of the men—not a new or remarkable thing either, where families do their own work. In general the old-timers, the foreman and the neighbors and their wives, were steadier and more knowledgeable than the younger paid hands, a couple of whom had a sort of dapper, mythic, rodeo look about them, at least to my outlander's eye. There was an exception, though, an unprepossessing specimen at first glance. He was in his twenties, scrawny and slightly stooped when afoot, with small darting close-set green eyes, a pointed nose, and a flow of frizzy red-blonde hair hanging down between his shoulders and sticking out over his ears. All his outer gear looked second- or third-hand, being worn and battered and soiled from use—scuffed boots with spurs, greasy scarred chaps, a stained and ripped down vest, and one of the more disastrous hats I've ever seen worn, filthy, its brim drooping down at an angle all around, with a home-made band of rattlesnake skin in which he'd stuck a tall frayed eagle feather. But the clothes next to his body were clean, and the wife of the man he worked for said with a smile that he washed that long hair every day. They called him, aptly, Wild Man, and I never heard his real name.

He watched me when I was around and dodged any talk, and I thought this was because I was an aging, alien non-cowboy till I noticed he was shy and short with all the others as well. He was also more skillful than any of them at the work that had to be done. Mounted, all his scrawniness went away and he was so tightly fluid and balanced that the old cliché about being part of the horse was wrong; instead the horse, whatever horse he was on, turned into a swift, strong, quick-turning part of him. He could think like a cow only faster, they said, and rope like a Mexican, and one evening when they came over the shoulder of a mountain with the three hundred or so steers they had gathered up that day, the Wild Man was not with them, showing up a little later from a different direction with fifteen beasts he was driving on his own. "They tore off up the worst canyon we got," the ranch's foreman said. "I knowed that funny-lookin' little son of a bitch was the only one I had could bring them things out by himself, and I needed everybody else to help with the main bunch."

He'd worked for one of the neighbor ranchers for three summer seasons so far, and within a couple of weeks now he would throw his bedroll and suitcase and saddle in the back of an old yellow pickup and take off for Arizona where on some ranch, they didn't know which, there was a winter job waiting. The rancher, a quiet man of sixty-five or so, said he was the best help they'd ever had, as deft and willing at building fences or constructing sheds and feeders as he was with horses and cows.

I asked if he did any rodeoing, because it was something most of those people seemed to talk about.

He shook his head. "I haven't got the least idea," he said. "You've seen for yourself what a talky scutter he is. I don't much think he likes all that stuff, though. What he likes is work, and getting things done right." He paused and spat tobacco juice and said, "Me, what I hope is old Wild Man just shows up next spring."

"Lord, I do too," said his wife with feeling.

And so for my own reasons, mythic or not, do I.

JOHN GRAVES

About the Photographer

Ray Rector was born on November 23, 1884, in the little village of Indian Gap, Hamilton County, Texas. His father, W. S. Rector, was a Tennessee Civil War veteran who had come to Texas in 1873. Ray was just an infant when the family moved to a farm near Roby in Fisher County, northwest of Abilene, where Ray's father became surveyor, county clerk, farmer, and dairy cattleman.

While still a teenager, Ray answered the call heard by many young men and boys of his time and left home to work as a cowboy on the high-plains ranches of the Texas Panhandle. As a cowhand on the vast XIT ranch of that region, he took part in several cattle drives. Later, after a short experience of working in the fruit industry in California, Ray became ill with malaria. Homesickness and a desire to return to a more healthful climate brought him back to West Texas. It was in Stamford, Texas, in 1902 that Ray and his brother Glen acquired the equipment—cameras and darkroom supplies—of a photographer named Higginbotham, who also taught the young men everything he knew about the craft of taking and developing photographs.

After a short period in business together as Rector & Rector, the brothers separated; Glen, succumbing to the lure of the West, moved to California. Ray continued the operation in Stamford, making portraits and taking popular photographs of the events of the bustling young farm and ranch supply center—the coming of the railroad, cir-

cus parades, church socials, and street scenes. Yet probably the part of his photography that he enjoyed most was on those occasions when he visited the ranches of northwest Texas, where he photographed scenes of ranch life and cowboys at work and at play. With a portable Kodak Autograph camera ever in hand, he relived his cowboy days and made many friends among those still actively engaged in the cattle industry.

Most of Rector's cowboy pictures were made on the Flat Top, Spur, and Throckmorton divisions of the S. M. Swenson, or SMS, ranches, organized by 1882 eventually to comprise some three hundred thousand acres, but he often visited other ranches as well—those of the Baldwins and Mayfields near Aspermont, the Colberts near Lueders, the Batemans near Benjamin, and the Pattersons in Kent and Stonewall counties, for example. Always his interest was in the everyday activities and entertainments of the ranchers and cowhands.

Rector was also active in the community affairs of Stamford. He was an active worker in the Methodist Church, the Rotary Club, the school board, and several fraternal organizations, including the Independent Order of Odd Fellows, for which he served as Texas Grand Master in 1931, the Woodmen of the World, the Modern Woodmen, and the Red Men. He organized the first troop in Texas of what was later to become the Boy Scouts of America, and he enlisted as a private in the Texas Militia and rose to the rank of captain. He gave of his time and energy to direct the United Charities for the community during the early years of the depression. He conceived the idea of, and helped to establish, a cowboy reunion that would perpetuate the memory of the West; bring together old-time ranchers and cowhands for a few days of fellowship, reminiscence, and entertainment; and keep alive the traditions of those who had wrested a life from the land and cattle. Largely as a result of his idea and efforts, the first Texas Cowboy Reunion was held in Stamford in 1930. It continues each year in July as the largest cowboy get-together and amateur rodeo in the world and one of the state's great attractions.

Ray Rector always remained proud of his West Texas heritage, and realizing that someday the era of the cowboy would be gone, he spoke of his photographs as a means of preserving that era. It would have been his wish that they be shared and enjoyed by others.

Today, most of the photographs in these pages, and nearly one thousand more negatives and prints, are housed in the Humanities Research Center at the University of Texas at Austin, placed there in 1979 by Margaret Rector, a daughter. Many of the photographs reproduced here were made available by Roy Flukinger, curator of photography, and the other staff members of the center. Other photographs and the details in the captions were provided by Margaret Rector and Tommy Rector, Ray's son, who continues the photographic studio in Stamford.

Cowboy Life on the Texas Plains

Ray Rector and his cow pony about 1930. Having worked on the XIT and other ranches as a teenager, Rector had a fond attachment to the cowboy's way of life. He knew that someday the era of the cowboy would be gone, and he spoke of his pictures as a means of preserving that passing way of life.

The Swenson Ranch took pride in their fine stock of cow ponies. The breed was from Spanish or Mexican herds. They were small and quick and had plenty of cow sense. They were well suited to ranch work by instinct and required little training. Here, wranglers move the remuda on the open range of the Flat Top branch of the SMS.

The remuda was the herd of horses from which those to be used for the day's work were chosen. Each cowboy had several horses that were considered his property. He named them all and used them in performing his job.

On the range a rope was used as a "corral" to contain the remuda. Horses were range-fed in the early days. A horse wrangler was in charge of the remuda and was responsible for seeing that they were properly grazed and watered.

Cowboys picking out their mounts for the day. Some of the early SMS Ranch horses were given names like Puddin' Foot, Boll Weevil, Clabber, and Pole Cat. The cowboys were great on nicknames for horses as well as for people.

Saddling horses on the SMS. A horse was usually ridden for several hours at a time, then rested and not ridden again for a day or so. There was a great deal of love and respect between the cowboy and his mount.

Picking out the horses. The cowboy in the center is wearing an extra-wide-brimmed "ten-gallon" hat for protection from the sun. Rarely was a cowboy seen without his hat.

Throwing a loop to catch a horse. Cowboys knew to walk quietly among the horses to lasso their mounts and to avoid scattering the herd.

Catching a skittish horse. The small, wiry Spanish cow horses were known for their speed and endurance. They had a little meanness in them, yet with proper breeding they were unequaled in producing a good remuda for ranch work.

It is told that this cowboy, called "Six," came from the famous Four Sixes (6666) Ranch near Guthrie, Texas, to work for the SMS. Cowboys were better known by their nicknames than by their real names. Six carries his riggin', a cowboy's prized possessions.

Saddling a mount. Keeping a spirited horse still long enough to saddle up was not always a simple matter. The cowboy in this picture appears to be in control at the moment.

The remuda and a tall, lean cowboy, Elvis Hines, saddling his mount. The cowboy's dress was high-heeled boots, a ten-gallon hat, a red bandana, and a blue denim shirt with a pocket full of Bull Durham makin's. Leather chaps worn over ducking britches were protection while riding through the rough and thorny mesquite brush.

In the dusty corral. Horses and riders seemed to thrive on the ever-present red West Texas dust. Not a sprig of grass can be seen where these men and animals stir up the powdery earth.

This cowboy has caught his horse, but he still has a job ahead of him before he can get mounted. Though the cowboys' work was not easy, many would not have traded their dawn-to-dusk days for any other way of life.

Readying the horses for work. The Swenson Ranch purchased a herd of Spanish mares in the 1880's to start their herd. These horses are descendants of the original breeding band.

Skittery cow ponies anxious to leave the corral. Certain cowboys were especially adept at riding the newly broken horses and soon gained fame for their ability to handle the "outlaws."

Buster Lee, a famous SMS bronc rider, on an outlaw horse about 1929.

Bronc buster Cleo Shipman taking a rough ride. His nearby companion, Roy Phillips, has a lasso ready to catch the horse if help becomes necessary.

Saddled horses wait quietly in a corral at the SMS Throckmorton Ranch about 1925.

These Flat Top Ranch cowhands have just ridden in from spring branding, reeking of the smoke of branding pens and sweaty leather.

Leland Seifres and Bill Maddox stretch a lariat rope. Hemp ropes when new were stiff, and it was necessary to break them in to make them pliable and easier to use for roping.

Left to right: Ray Rector, cowboy photographer; Mr. Andrew John Swenson; and one of Swenson's sons, Rudolph, about 1929. Mr. "A. J.," a native of Sweden, became the great and be- loved general manager of the Swenson ranches. Rudolph ran the Pitchfork Ranch until his death in 1942.

"Scandalous" John Selmon, a picturesque character on his paint horse, was SMS Flat Top Ranch foreman. Scandalous John once described how he got his nickname: "It was May of 1900, an ole horse named Towelface bucked me off! When I got up, I said, he's a scan'lous buckin' son of a gun! and then I got on him and rode him" (Gail Swenson, M.A. thesis, University of Texas, 1960; Gail's father was A. M. G. "Swede" Swenson).

Jake Raines, SMS old-timer and favorite among the cowboys. Jake was widely known and respected in ranching circles and truly typical of the early-day cowboy. This photograph was made about 1914.

Cattle being herded to a watering hole. Surface tanks like this one were man-made and dependent on rains to keep them filled. Water was always a problem in West Texas, and ranchers suffered through critical drought periods. These tanks were needed in great numbers to meet the demands of large-scale cattle operations.

A cattle herd out on the range. The Hereford breed was originally imported from England. Texas ranchers cross-bred the Shorthorn and the Whiteface to develop the successful herds on most West Texas ranches.

Loading cattle to be shipped to northern markets about 1929. Cattle were driven to pens located near a railroad siding to be loaded onto cattle cars. Townships were created as railroads were built in this area to serve the cattle industry.

Roping calves for branding. This scene is from the Mayfield ranch near Aspermont, Texas, about 1925.

A young cowboy in a predicament. He has roped a faunchin'
calf, but as he is dismounting, his saddle is turning.

Bringing down a calf for branding. The camera stops the action of the calf and rope in mid-air. This is a remarkable shot, since Rector used a Kodak hand-held camera with film of very low speed. The picture was taken about 1927.

John Selmon has roped a calf, but the "flanker" has more than he can handle. Both man and calf eat the dust in this effort to tie down the animal.

Cowboys look on as a calf is thrown for branding. Tony Selmon,
son of John Selmon, is the lad on horseback.

Branding the SMS at the Throckmorton Ranch about 1927. In addition to application of the branding iron, other necessary chores at the same time included doctoring for screwworms, de-horning, castrating, vaccinating, and ear marking. "Shoofly" horn paint was swabbed on after dehorning.

In this branding scene the irons are heated over a mesquite fire
at the right. A hot iron smokes as the calf's hair is burned off.

Weatherby's Hole, a watering place on the SMS Flat Top Ranch,
about 1920.

A remuda watering at Weatherby's Hole about 1928.

This watering hole is a serene spot for both men and horses.
The animals look fat and sleek from good range grazing.

Mayfield Ranch cowboys stop for rest and to water their horses
at a large rain-filled tank.

This chuckwagon is loaded with provisions and on its way to the cow camp. The driver is Lee Kelly, an SMS cook noted for his famous and delicious sourdough biscuits. The horses were named Booger, Red, Chico, and Stud.

At the camping ground, chuckwagon boss Lee Kelly (left, with apron and cup) has prepared the traditional cowboy fare over an open mesquite wood fire. Other familiar ranch men pictured here are (*left to right*) Doc Gustavson (with pipe), Roy Phillips, and Rudolph Swenson. Note the bedrolls lying about. On the range the cowboys slept on the ground underneath the stars.

A black cook called "Sooner" on the Flat Top Ranch prepares a cowboy breakfast. Strong black coffee, thick slices from a bacon side, biscuits, and gravy were the usual fare for starting the day. The cook's helper was a young hired hand called the "hoodlum," who did menial chores until he was experienced enough to be a regular cowboy. He also drove the hoodlum wagon, which was used to carry various supplies for the camp and the cowboys' bedrolls.

Lee Kelly, the "Sourdough King," at his chuckwagon. Kelly was one of those cooks who would "yell 'come 'n get it,' and then squat on the shady side of the wagon to clean the dough from their fingernails and roll a cigarette" (John Hendrix, "A Comin Four Year Old," *Texas Cowboy Reunion Program*, July, 1933). The hoodlum wagon is shown at the right.

Fritz Cordium, chuckwagon cook, stirs some food cooking in an iron pot. The fire was built in a pit, and iron rods were laid across the pit to hold the heavy cooking pots. A five-gallon lard can was used for heating water to wash the dishes (tin cups and plates).

A cow camp with a chuckwagon and a water wagon. Streams of running water were scarce on the SMS ranch. A metal tank with wooden ends mounted on iron wheels always went along with the chuckwagon. Water was used for cooking, drinking, dishwashing, and washing of hands and faces, but not for bathing.

Cowboys "hunker," or sit on the ground, to eat. The menu was simple but nourishing, and the food was generally good—depending on the mood of the cook. Cowboys didn't complain if they didn't like the fare.

A cowboy eating at the chuckwagon on the SMS Flat Top Ranch about 1920. The Dutch oven at right cooks sourdough biscuits. Coals of fire are placed on top of the lid to brown the biscuits on top. Such baking was a real art in breadmaking.

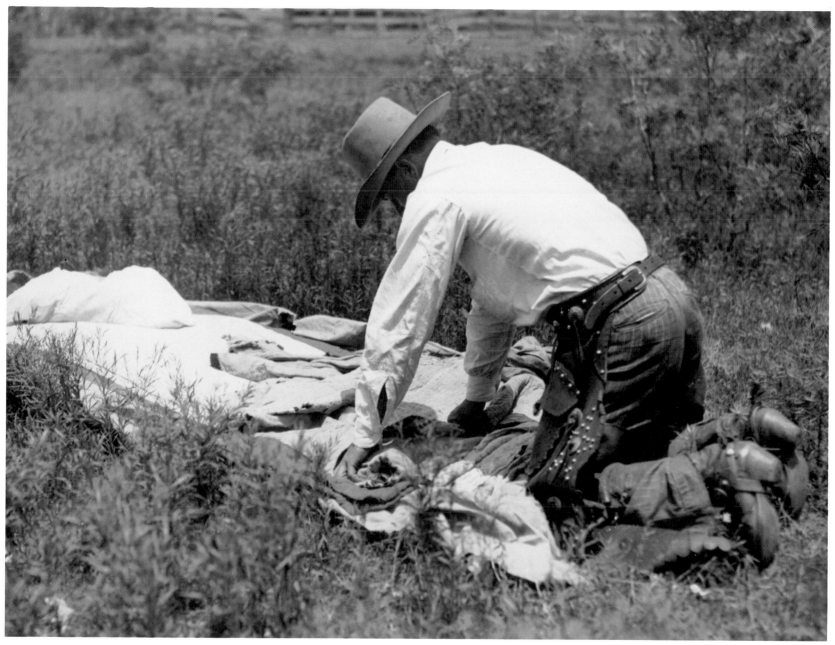

Cowboy Ted Cravens making up his bedroll on the SMS Flat Top
about 1920.

The country in which the cowboys worked. This scene is along
the Wichita River on the Bateman Ranch near Benjamin, Texas,
about 1931.

Ranch hands gather under the shade of the wagon sheet covering the chuckwagon for a friendly card game about 1925. After a hearty noonday meal out on the open range, the cowboys enjoyed this brief rest from the roundup chores. A. J. Swenson, ranch boss, is seated at right on the barrel. A hindquarter of beef hangs in a screened box on the left.

A rope artist twirls a lariat. Cowboys prided themselves in their skills with a rope. Most were experts with the lasso at roping cattle and horses. Here, the cowboy called "Six" shows off with a fancy running noose about 1927.

Four cowhands in a washer pitching contest. Simple games like this were a popular means of recreation when time permitted. No doubt some good wagering took place also. The chuckwagon in the background indicates that this was an after-dinner pastime. Cowboys ate dinner at noontime. The evening meal was supper.

A cow pony race. A ranch hand usually had the use of more than one horse, and the cowboy had a favorite mount that he liked to use to prove his skill as a good horseman. The cow pony was a real workhorse, not bred for speed but for stamina and good cow sense.

Miss Breland, a schoolteacher from a nearby ranching community, was one of the visitors from the surrounding area who often came to the ranches on special occasions. A ranch boss would sometimes arrange a party for the single cowboys to get acquainted with eligible ladies. This was a welcomed social event, for the cowboys working out on the range may not have seen a lady for days. There was always dancing to fiddle music and lots of good food. Matchmaking was not uncommon. This photograph was made about 1914.

Cowboys and ladies gathered around the chuckwagon for a posed picture. Note the cook in his white flour sack apron. This may have been Sunday dinner at the camp during a roundup. The ladies often brought some of their own cooking, such as pies with meringue on top, which the cowboys called "calf slobber." Cakes and pies brought to a cow camp were welcomed treats. A. J. Swenson, general manager of the SMS ranches, is on the far right.

This chuckwagon scene shows the cook, Ross Kinchloe, preparing the meal. A typical menu would be "son-of-a-gun" (stew), beans, sourdough biscuits, stewed dried fruit such as apples and apricots, and strong boiled coffee. Kinchloe had a reputation as a fine cook. Cowhands were hearty eaters, but few suffered from obesity. Jake Raines, a well-known cowman, is at far right. The others, left to right, are Joe Ericson, "Poss" Murray, "Nig" Clary, Pete Holcombe, Miss Breland, Ross Kinchloe, and another lady schoolteacher.

Cook Ross Kinchloe serves the visiting ladies along with "Nig" Clary and Pete Holcombe, SMS cowboys. The chuck box, built on the rear of the wagon, carried provisions for meals. The table was hinged to close when all supplies and utensils were stored away. The famous trail driver Charles Goodnight is believed to have been the inventor of the chuck box.

A chuckwagon on the Flat Top Ranch, a division of the vast S. M. Swenson ranches near Stamford, is shown here about 1927. Mamie Rector, wife of the photographer, and Scandalous John Selmon, Flat Top foreman, talk near the fires. A canvas tarpaulin, or wagon sheet, was stretched over the chuckwagon to afford shade from the blistering West Texas sun. Trees were scarce and generally were mesquite, which gave little shade but made excellent firewood for camp cooking. The tepee-style tent at left was a luxury not usually found in a cow camp.

Lady visitors help wash dishes at a Flat Top camp about 1931. Tin plates and cups were always used. There were no paper dishes or cups in those days. The cook was always happy to be relieved of dishwashing chores.

Vira Owen and Mary Reeves listen to a yarn from Scandalous John Selmon. The ladies were avid square dancers and usually were able to organize a lively session of dancing with cowboys.

Do-si-do and swing your partner. Dancers didn't have to wait until dark to enjoy square dancing on a wagon sheet. A cloudless West Texas sky beams over all. Music was from fiddle and guitar players. This dance was on the Mayfield Ranch about 1927. The bowed legs of the cowboy in the foreground attest to many years in the saddle.

Here, square dancing livens up a cow camp when cowboys and their ladies take time to enjoy their favorite recreation. Though this photo, from about 1930, appears to be made at mid-day, they danced anytime the opportunity was at hand. Guitar and fiddle music set the tempo. The wagon sheet kept the dry, powdery earth from creating clouds of dust from the dancers' feet.

John Selmon, Flat Top Ranch foreman, washes a lady's face, or perhaps removes some dust from her eye, at the water wagon.

Scenes like this show that it was not "all work and no play" for the cowboy.

A hack (short for "hackney") was the horse-drawn taxi of the early 1900's. Here, a driver repairs a broken wheel. The hack carried passengers for a fare or could be hired for trips between towns. Roads were usually trails across the prairies. Curtains of canvas could be dropped from the sides of the roof to protect passengers from dust, wind, and rain.

Cowboys gather at a ranch house. Such houses were built of lumber with little emphasis on luxury. Note the wash bench with tubs next to house. Laundry was done outside and hung on barbed-wire fences to dry. Near the foreman's house is a bunk-house where the cowhands slept. Running water, electricity, and indoor plumbing were not available. Cooking inside was done on iron stoves that burned mesquite wood.

The Spur Ranch headquarters as it appeared in the early 1920's. In its prime the Spur, or Espuela, was one of the largest and best-known West Texas ranches. E. P. and S. A. Swenson purchased it in 1906, not primarily for ranching but for coloniza- tion. A railroad was built to run eighty-three miles from Stamford to the ranch, and ranch property was sold to settlers; the venture was an outstanding success. The Swenson interests retained a portion of the ranch, which they operated until 1970.

The Mayfield ranch house near Aspermont was the home of a prominent West Texas ranching family in the mid-1920's. The house is typical of the era. A cistern, seen near the right end of the house, collected rain that fell on the roof and was carried by gutters into the deep well. Water was then drawn out by a bucket and pulley rope. Note the vegetable garden enclosed by a fence. At the left can be seen the cowboys' bunkhouse. Lightning rods, common on houses of the period, were fastened to the gables to ground lightning bolts that might strike the house.

Saddles on a corral fence at the SMS Flat Top Ranch about 1928. Next to his horse, a cowboy's saddle was his most prized possession. There were many fine saddle makers in the West Texas ranch country who crafted saddles to order and decorated them with hand-tooled designs. A good saddle cost from $37 to $50 in the early 1920's. A cowboy spent the greater part of his days in a saddle, so it was a very important piece of his gear.

A very small boy on a big horse. Children on ranches learned to ride at a very early age. The saddle is a small child's size, but the youngster looks a bit apprehensive as though this might be his first time to ride such a big horse. The man on horseback in the background may be the proud father.

Young Tony Selmon, son of John Selmon, learned the ways of ranching from his father. He later chose a career of medicine and is currently a practicing physician and surgeon in Stamford.

Baldwin ranch house near Aspermont. This building was the courthouse at Rayner, Texas, original seat of Stonewall County. The county seat was later moved to Aspermont, and the Baldwin family bought this building for their home. It still stands and is a landmark in its area.

The railroad comes to Stamford. At the turn of the century the Texas Central Railroad was established to ship cattle from this West Texas area. Land out of the Swenson Ranch was set aside and given for the new townsite of Stamford.

Downtown Stamford after a good soaking rain about 1900. The town was named for Stamford, Connecticut, the home of the president of the Texas Central Railroad. Established primarily for ranching interests, it also soon became a thriving agricultural center as land came into cultivation.

Wagons and horses around City Hall Square and Patillo Hardware about 1903. The town grew and prospered, and in 1907 Stamford College was founded by the Methodist Church. In 1920 the college burned and was reestablished in Abilene as part of McMurry College.

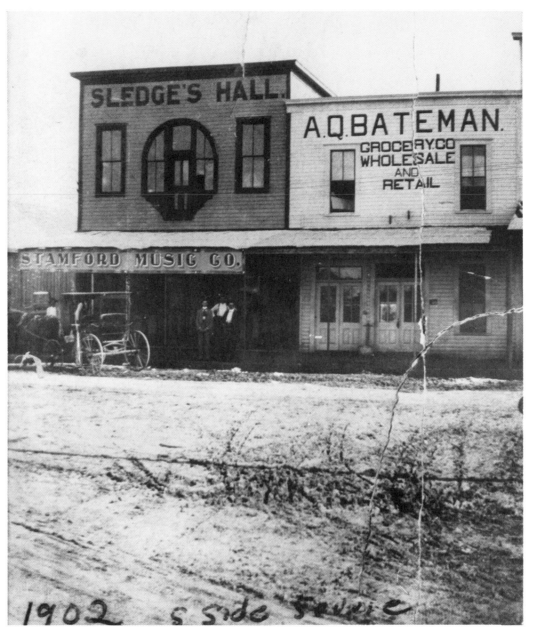

1902 S side Fowler

Sledge's Hall and Bateman Grocery and Hardware Store, popular business establishments about 1905. The hall was used for social gatherings, lodge meetings, and community entertainment and was owned and operated by Dr. J. R. Sledge, one of the town's first physicians.

Another view of the growing town of Stamford about 1903. Circus tents can be seen in the upper right of this picture. The Sells-Floto show visited Stamford in the early days as the town became a supply center for surrounding cattle raisers and farmers. There were about three thousand inhabitants at that time.

A horse-and-buggy street scene in Stamford about 1905. The cowboys from the outlying ranches came here on Saturdays to kick up their heels.

The camp meeting at a country church or on the banks of the Clear Fork of the Brazos River near Stamford was a tradition and custom of the pioneers—an annual summertime get-to-gether for folks from all of the neighboring communities. Fam-ilies came and camped for several days to hear the gospel preached, enjoy singing, and visit with old friends. The group photograph, this one from about 1905, was an occasion when the ladies and gents dressed in their Sunday best.

A rodeo parade moves around the square in Stamford. The Texas Cowboy Reunion had its first celebration in June, 1930. Opening-day festivities began with a large parade of bands, cowboys on horseback, chuckwagons, and floats. The purpose of the celebration was to welcome back the cowboys of the 1880's and 1890's who gathered to reminisce and live over the days when Stamford was a roundup ground.

The Sweetwater chuckwagon rides in a Cowboy Reunion parade about 1930. Surrounding towns participated in the parade with wagons and floats depicting the cowboy life.

Grand entry at a performance of the Texas Cowboy Reunion rodeo in Stamford in the early thirties. The arena was filled with hundreds of riders, who were mostly contestants in the rodeo events. The Texas Cowboy Reunion is known today throughout the world as the largest gathering of true working cowboys, and the rodeo is one of the largest amateur rodeos in America.

Presenting the colors at the opening ceremonies of the Cowboy Reunion rodeo in its early days. The governor of Texas usually attended, as did Texas Rangers and many other dignitaries. En-tertainers like Will Rogers and Paul Whiteman were guests at early-day reunions.

Rodeo contestants gather to begin an event, probably calf roping. Among other events were wild cow milking, bronc riding, bull riding, and cutting horse contests. The contestants were real working cowboys from the ranches of the area.

Judging the calf roping contest. The flagman on horseback keeps a flag raised until the roper has thrown and securely tied the calf. John Lindsay, the clown, played an important part in the arena events by helping lure mean horses and bulls away from fallen riders.

BUCK HAWKINS on CANDYWAGON

Buck Hawkins, a famous bronc rider, is up on Candywagon, an
ornery and notorious piece of horse flesh.

The Swenson Throckmorton Ranch chuckwagon sets up camp at the Texas Cowboy Reunion. Each outfit brought its own wagon for its cowboys, who ate and slept there during the three-day celebration.

Old-time cattlemen at the Cowboy Reunion. In addition to taking part in rodeo events for cowboys over fifty-five years of age, the old-timers found the reunion to be a special time to renew old acquaintances, swap stories, and talk of the good ol' days.

Walt Cousins, Cowboy Reunion historian, wrote, "They were hell-bustin', God fearing men who used to know the lonesome cattle country."

An old-timer shows off his first-prize award of a fine saddle, won in a roping contest. This veteran cowboy is typical of the men who still come each year to the Cowboy Reunion in Stamford.

A veteran cowhand at the SMS Throckmorton Ranch, known only as "Tige," proudly wears his old-timer's badge to show that he has been cowboying for many years.

Texas Rangers were special guests at the Texas Cowboy Reunion about 1931. Left to right are John Selmon, a Ranger, an old-time cattleman, and Tom Hickman, a former captain of the Rangers.

The Rangers were not at the reunion to keep law and order but to relax and enjoy the get-together of ranch folks during this annual celebration.